Pet Care

A CAT FOR YOU

Caring for Your Cat

Written by Susan Blackaby

Illustrated by Charlene DeLage

Content Advisers: Jennifer Zablotny, D.V.M.
Kerrie Burns, D.V.M.
Reading Adviser: Susan Kesselring, M.A., Literacy Educator
Rosemount-Apple Valley-Eagan (Minnesota) School District

PiCTURE WiNDOW BOOKS
Minneapolis, Minnesota

Editor: Nadia Higgins

Designer: Nathan Gassman

Page production: Picture Window Books

The illustrations in this book were painted with watercolor.

Picture Window Books

5115 Excelsior Boulevard

Suite 232

Minneapolis, MN 55416

1-877-845-8392

www.picturewindowbooks.com

Printed in the United States of America.

1 2 3 4 5 6 08 07 06 05 04 03

Library of Congress Cataloging-in-Publication Data

Blackaby, Susan.

A cat for you : caring for your cat / written by Susan Blackaby ; illustrations by Charlene DeLage.

v. cm. — (Pet care)

Contents: Cats as pets—Feeding your cat—Cat moods—Cat care—What your cat needs—The cat's meow—Fun facts—Kinds of cats.

ISBN 1-4048-0115-4 (lib. bdg.)

1. Cats—Juvenile literature. [1. Cats.] 1. DeLage, Charlene, 1944-ill. II. Title.

SF447 .B54 2003

636.8'0887—dc21

2002154999

TABLE OF CONTENTS

Cats as Pets

People have had cats as pets for more than 4,000 years.
Maybe a cat is the pet for you!

Cats can live in the city or the country.
Taking care of a pet cat is pretty easy.

Feeding Your Cat

Cats are meat eaters.

Farm cats eat mice, birds, and other small animals.

House cats need to eat cat food.

Cat food has the things your cat needs to stay healthy.

Cats can be very fussy about their food.

You will need to find food your cat likes.

You might have to try a few different kinds.

Some cats do not like cold food.

Let food from the fridge warm up before you give it to your cat.

Never give your cat raw meat or raw fish.

Give your cat plenty of fresh water.

Keep your cat's food and water dishes clean.

Cat Moods

Happy cats close their eyes till they are almost shut.
They turn their ears back. They purr.

Angry cats raise their ears and turn them back.

The black spot in the center of their eyes gets small.

Scared cats open their eyes wide.

The black spot in the center of their eyes gets big.

woof!

Are your cat's eyes open wide?
Are its ears pointy?
It wants to play!

Cat Care

Cats like to keep themselves clean. You can help.

Brush your cat every day.

Brushing gets rid of dirt and dust.

Long-haired cats need extra brushing.
Their silky fur gets mats and tangles.

Cats need to keep their claws short and sharp.

Get your cat a scratching post.

Cats need to keep fit.

Get your cat some toys to play with.

Cats need to go to the bathroom.

Train your cat to use a litter box.

Clean the box once a day.

Replace the kitty litter once a week.

Take your cat to the vet for checkups.
Your vet will help keep your cat healthy.

See your vet if your cat is too fat or too thin.

See your vet if your cat has no zip.

Signs of a healthy cat:

- Shiny coat
- Bright eyes
- Dry nose
- Pink gums

 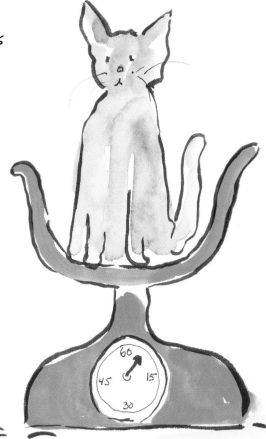

What Your Cat Needs

Cats need lots of fresh air and sunshine.

Cats need lots of time alone.

Cats need lots of exercise and plenty of sleep.

How Kitty Spends Its Day	
Eat	1 hour
Rest	2 hours
Play	2 hours
Hunt	1 hour
Cuddle	1 hour
Nap	4 hours
Explore	1 hour
Sleep	12 hours

Cats need lots and lots of love.

Give your cat these things.

Your cat will be the purr-fect pet.

The Cat's Meow

Draw pictures to go with these sayings.

You are the cat's pajamas!

Has the cat got your tongue?

Don't let the cat out of the bag.

A cat has nine lives.

Fun Facts

- Cats have 24 whiskers. There are four rows on each side. Cats use their whiskers as feelers.
- A cat can fit through any opening the size of its head.
- Ancient Egyptians tamed cats to keep snakes and mice out of their homes.
- A cool, wet nose is a sign of a healthy cat. Sick cats often have warm, dry noses.
- The cat family has big, wild cats and small, domestic (tame) cats. Most of the big cats, like lions and tigers, can roar but cannot purr. The small cats can purr but cannot roar.

Words to Know

checkup—a visit to the vet to make sure your cat is healthy

litter box—a special box where a cat can go to the bathroom

scratching post—a short pole, covered with rope or carpeting, that gives a cat something good to scratch

vet (short for veterinarian)—a doctor who treats animals

22

Kinds of Cats

Most of the cats that people own are a mix of different breeds. Some of these cats have names that describe the patterns on their fur.

Name	What they look like
Calico	A calico cat is white with orange and black patches.
Tabby	A tabby cat has stripes like a tiger's.
Tortoiseshell	A tortoiseshell cat is black with orange and cream patches.
Tuxedo	A tuxedo cat has a black back and a white belly and chest.

Pure breeds each have their own look and way of acting. Here are just a few.

Name	What they look like	How they act
Cornish Rex	Has curly hair	Is very active
Manx	Has no tail	Is smart and fun
Persian	Has long, glossy fur	Is quiet and tidy
Sphynx	Has no fur	Is affectionate and loyal
Siamese	Is slim and sleek	Is very talkative

To Learn More

At the Library

Frost, Helen. *Cats*. Mankato, Minn.: Pebble Books, 2001.

George, Jean Craighead. *How to Talk to Your Cat*. New York: HarperCollins, 2000.

Miller, Virginia. *Be Gentle!* Cambridge, Mass.: Candlewick Press, 1997.

Rylant, Cynthia. *Mr. Putter and Tabby Feed the Fish*. San Diego: Harcourt, 2001.

On the Web

ASPCA Kids' Site
http://www.animaland.org
For stories, games, and information about pets

Cat Fanciers' Association
http://www.cfainc.org
For information about different breeds of cats
and how to care for them

Want to learn more about cats?
Visit FACT HOUND at *http://www.facthound.com*.

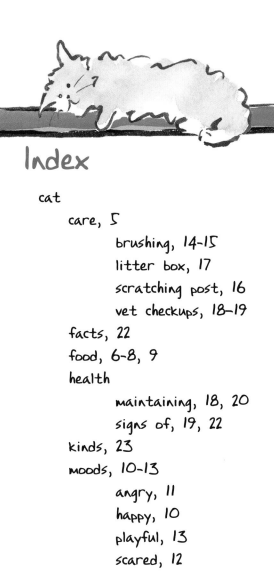

Index